Early Imperial Romans

Early Imperial Romans

Painting Wargaming Figures

Andy Singleton

Foreword by Dr Simon Elliott

Pen & Sword

MILITARY

AN IMPRINT OF PEN & SWORD BOOKS LTD.
YORKSHIRE ~ PHILADELPHIA

First published in Great Britain in 2019 by
Pen & Sword Military
An imprint of
Pen & Sword Books Ltd
Yorkshire – Philadelphia

ISBN 978 1 52671 635 4

A CIP catalogue record for this book is available from the British Library.

Typeset in Gill Sans 12/16 by Aura Technology and Software Services, India

Printed and bound in India by Replika Press Pvt. Ltd.

Pen & Sword Books Limited incorporates the imprints of Atlas, Archaeology, Aviation, Discovery, Family History, Fiction, History, Maritime, Military, Military Classics, Politics, Select, Transport, True Crime, Air World, Frontline Publishing, Leo Cooper, Remember When, Seaforth Publishing, The Praetorian Press, Wharncliffe Local History, Wharncliffe Transport, Wharncliffe True Crime and White Owl.

For a complete list of Pen & Sword titles please contact

PEN & SWORD BOOKS LIMITED
47 Church Street, Barnsley, South Yorkshire, S70 2AS, England
E-mail: enquiries@pen-and-sword.co.uk
Website: www.pen-and-sword.co.uk

Or
PEN AND SWORD BOOKS
1950 Lawrence Rd, Havertown, PA 19083, USA
E-mail: Uspen-and-sword@casematepublishers.com
Website: www.penandswordbooks.com

Contents

Acknowledgements

I'd like to extend my deepest thanks to all those friends and family who have encouraged and supported me in writing this book, but I'd like to single out John, Simon and Sarah especially for helping this book come to life.

Foreword

The Roman legionary of the Principate Empire was the elite fighting soldier of the ancient world. When clad in his helmet and banded iron armour, and carrying his rectangular body shield, lead-weighted javelins and vicious stabbing sword, his image symbolizes the might of the Roman Empire.

Yet the story of how this mighty warrior rose to the pinnacle of martial prowess is far more complex than commonly thought. It reflects the Roman trait for assimilating their opponent's best military technology and tactics. This, together with the Roman propensity for 'grit' in never giving up, meant that those who stood toe-to-toe with the Roman legionary on the battlefield were brave indeed, or foolish.

By the time of the Principate the panoply of the legionary had evolved through at least five changes to the core Roman military system. The first elite soldiers in the armies of Rome were the Etrusco-Roman hoplites of the Tullian First Class, these changing to the *hastati*, *principes* and *triarii* of the Camillan legions after the humiliating defeat by the Gauls at the Battle of Allia and subsequent sacking of Rome in 390 BC. This system evolved once more into the Polybian system after the Romans fought their first Hellenistic opponent, Pyrrhus of Epirus and his pike phalanx and elephants, in the early third century BC. The next major change was that of Marius in 107 BC at the height of the Cimbrian War, when the legions again found themselves losing badly to 'barbarians' from the North. This reform set the template for the later Principate legionary, all such troopers now equipped in the same way with a *lorica hamata* chainmail hauberk, scutum shield, a helmet increasingly based on those worn by the Gauls, two *pila* lead-weighted javelins and *gladius hispania* sword. The final reform into the Principate was that of the first emperor, Augustus, himself. Though this

was largely to do with the number of legions he deployed (around thirty at this time), it is from this time we see the legionaries wearing what has come to symbolize his *lorica segmentata* armour.

Thus we see that the legionary was a warrior who was constantly evolving to face each new threat, with the Romans always taking note of their greatest opponents and learning from the experience. In this way, even when the soldiers of the Principate were defeated in an individual engagement, they always came to ultimately be victorious. This is why they were the pre-eminent soldiers of antiquity.

Dr Simon Elliott

Tools of the Trade

Rome wasn't built in a day, and just like ancient civilizations, we need to cover some basics. At first glance (and a fair few later glances too), the array of tools, glues, paints and techniques varies between staggering and simply overwhelming. To help you begin to make some sense of this, I'll give a quick overview of some of the essentials, and what they can bring to your hobby sessions.

With such a huge range of paints and tools on the market, I can't include them all, but I'll cover some of the more popular ones. I'll try to cut through some of the technical terminology too, and at least give a description of what is required for a few of the most commonly used techniques.

Broadly speaking, with any tools you're better off buying better quality and, unfortunately by extension, more expensive tools, as in the vast majority of cases you really do get what you pay for. It's generally worth checking out a few reviews online, or asking around first, to get an idea of how the item performs in the real world.

PLASTIC, METAL OR RESIN?

Wargaming figures are supplied in several different materials, with plastic, metal and, to a far lesser extent, resin (though resin is common for terrain, and can also be used for larger models, such as elephants).

Plastic figures are typically provided on a frame, called a sprue, from which they need to be removed. Traditionally, 20mm plastic figures often come in a soft, polythene type of plastic. These require a vigorous scrubbing with warm water and washing-up liquid before painting. Thankfully, this is becoming less prevalent, and modern miniatures are increasingly produced in hard plastic, which is far less prone to warping, has better adhesion for paint and is lighter for storage purposes too. The 28mm figures are most commonly a hard plastic, though there

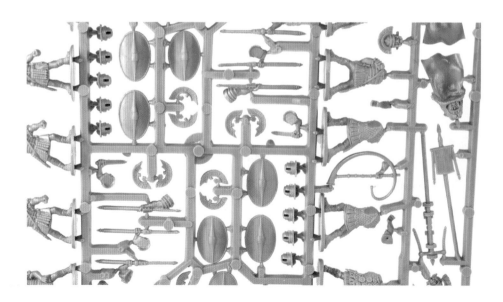

are also several hard plastic 20mm ranges, and soon too at least one 15mm range. The majority of 28mm figure manufacturers provide each figure in several pieces to allow you some variety in posing of the figures; I'll go into more detail of assembling these a little later.

Probably the most common material for the production of wargames figures, however, is lead-free metal. These are usually supplied as single-piece castings, and typically come with a small stand attached to the figure's feet to aid placing them on their bases. Both plastic and metal figures can have moulding lines along their sides and bases, as a by-product of the production process, that will need to be removed. This is a simple task and requires scraping along the line with the blunt side of a blade or quick sanding down with some files; again, I'll cover that a little later too.

Metal models require assembling with superglue or equivalent, and larger models such as artillery and cavalry will require a degree of patience as they can quickly become somewhat frustrating if you try to rush putting them together. When assembling any figure though, patience and test-fitting will always pay off here.

KNIVES, CUTTERS AND FILES

The first thing you'll need to do, unsurprisingly, is to get the component parts of your figure ready for assembly, and clean away any residue from the manufacturing process. This can take several forms, but the most common are flash and mould lines, which form when the model is being cast in its mould: these appear as either prominent lines around a figure, as chunks or 'worms' of excess material, especially on edges and undercuts of the figure. These casting imperfections can appear in any material, and removing them will massively improve the appearance of the finished model, especially when you are using the dry brush techniques.

Naturally, this requires some decent tools. I'd caution against using a machete and instead suggest getting some purpose-designed hobby tools instead. These can vary from prices too good to be true (and they generally are) to small fortunes.

Hobby knife

These broadly fall into two types: those with replaceable blades, such as the ubiquitous X-Acto hobby knife, and the Stanley knife. Either one of these will probably be your most frequently used tool in preparing your figures, as the sharp side of the blade can be used for cutting things, whilst the blunt (revolutionary!) edge can be used to remove mould lines by simply scraping it down them a few times.

Which type of knife you get is entirely up to you, but I'd recommend one of each, especially as they can be found for good prices pretty much anywhere that sells tools or hobby supplies. The replaceable

A knife being used for cleaning up excess plastic.

blades of the X-Acto style allow different styles and shapes of blade to be fitted, as well as allowing you to simply replace the blade once it becomes blunt. The slender, sharp blades do have their limits, however; they can blunt quickly when working with metal, and may struggle with cutting through thicker plastic sprues as well. For heavier duty work, the Stanley knife will do you good service, and is affordable enough to be disposable too.

Side cutters

Also known as sprue cutters, these are vaguely similar to scissors, but with a shorter blade and more powerful, tensioned action. As the name cunningly suggests, these are good at cutting things. Perfect for removing plastic parts from their carrying sprue, it's best to trim the part leaving a small stub of plastic that you can then trim with a knife or file. Also handy for metal, these can be used for removing casting lugs or parts from moulding blocks. Sprue cutters can be found in the majority of model shops, both on- and off-line.

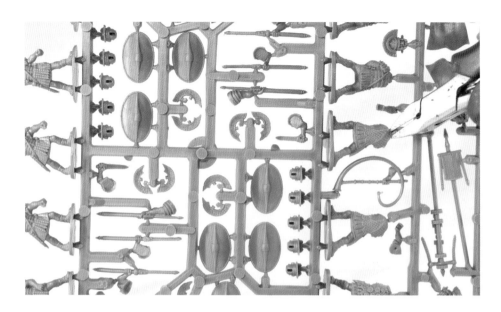

Files

Files are another immensely useful tool, and can be found in most tool/ hardware shops, as well as in model and hobby shops. Ideally, what you want is a set of jewellers' files, or needle files. These typically come in sets of several different files, with each being a different shape to allow

Using a file to remove some mould lines.

the cleaning of most parts of a model. A file with a blade more than a centimetre wide will probably prove to be too big for modelling purposes, so aim for something quite fine. These are great tools for removing mould lines and getting rid of the contact points of sprue gates.

GLUES

Now that we have established what the figure is made from, and have trimmed and cleaned the parts, it's time to start sticking things together. For this, we'll need to ensure we are matching the correct bonding agent to the right material. Very broadly speaking, the most commonly encountered glues are PVA, superglue, cement and solvent. PVA is a sticky

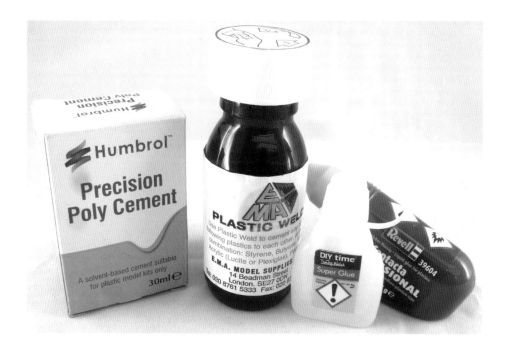

paste and fine for attaching the basing materials to your figure's bases, but is pretty useless for actually sticking your figures together.

Superglue, or Cyanoacrylate to give it its proper name, is a rapid-curing cement that bonds most materials. Given the rapidity of the bonding process, superglue works best when used in small, controlled areas. I tend to apply it with a cocktail stick or equivalent, and apply small dabs to each part that will be bonded. It's best to get the parts joined, and then come back and carefully add more superglue if you feel the bond needs it, than to flood an area that will take forever to dry, and potentially make a terrible mess of your model too.

Adhesives for plastics, such as those from Revell, Tamiya and Humbrol, are all solvent-based, to varying degrees, and have a fairly wide range of drying times. In addition, there are solvents designed with modelling in mind, such as Plastic Weld, which are far more potent products. All of these function off the basis of partially melting the two bonding surfaces of plastic into a very strong bond. They won't, however, bond metal, resin or plastic to metal or resin. For this you will still need superglue.

Finally, we have cements. These typically come supplied in tubes, and are very sticky and foul smelling. Whilst eventually they can give a decent bond, they are for the most part quite inferior to the purpose-designed adhesives already mentioned, and should probably be avoided.

PAINT AND PRIMER, AND SPRAY CANS

Now that our model is built, we can start to paint it. Before we can look at some techniques though, I should probably cover a few key types of paint and paint products on the market.

In most of these guides I will be referring to using primers and spray cans, especially for the first steps of each guide.

First off, primers are probably the most important type of paint you can get, especially when working with resin or metal. These differ from paint, in being specially formulated to give a hard-wearing coat that gives a resilient surface for handling and painting. With most paints for wargaming being water-based, this is especially important as repeated handling without a primer can cause paint to wear off a finished model. Primers typically come in black, white, grey and dark red, and I prefer to get them from places selling car body paints. If you have an airbrush, there are also a selection of good primers on the market for these, but time and space constraints mean I'll be avoiding discussing airbrushes in this book.

When working with purely plastic models, you can get away with using coloured spray paints as the initial layer of colour. There are a great many of these on the market, in both enamel and acrylic form, so finding something to fit your needs shouldn't be too hard. Notable ranges include The Army Painter, Plastic Soldier Company, Tamiya and Humbrol. When working with metal or resin models, I'd suggest applying a light coating of primer and allowing this to dry thoroughly (at least 12 hours, better for 24 though).

By far the vast majority of paints used for wargaming are acrylic. These are water soluble, but quick drying and hard wearing. Most paint when purchased, such as those from the Vallejo Model Colour range, require some thinning to get the best results, as paint that is too thick will not only be difficult to get where you want it to go, but may also swamp the detail on your model too. To thin your paint, simply apply a little paint to a pallet (an old tile or plastic lid is great for this), then add an equal amount of water and stir together using an old brush. For best results, add a tiny amount of flow improver, which will hold the coverage of the paint together well, whilst still keeping the paint controllable.

You may also encounter enamel paints. These are an oil-based product, and whilst useful, especially for basing and wreathing applications on vehicles, are of less use to us in getting our armies finished, as the drying times are considerably longer than with acrylics and they also require more specialized cleaning and thinning products.

PAINT BRUSHES AND CARE

So, with all this discussion of tools, I suppose paint brushes might be a good one to mention in a book on figure painting! As with most tools, brushes vary from super cheap, where you get a pack of a dozen brushes for a few pounds, up to fine Kolinsky sable brushes that can seem hugely expensive in comparison. As someone who paints a huge amount of models, it's worth splashing out on the best quality brushes you can afford, as not only will they last longer but they'll work out cheaper in the long term.

A high-quality brush will also give you better brush control and a finer finish. Personally, I predominantly use the Winsor and Newton series 7, Rosemary and Co and Broken Toad ranges. That said, for things like applying washes and dry brushing, I do find simple, cheap hobby brushes from the craft shop to be perfectly adequate. For less expensive though still serviceable brushes, Pro Arte, Army Painter and Games Workshop all produce useful brushes. Again though, it's worth having some cheap, disposable brushes too for jobs like mixing paint, applying washes, dry brushing and applying glue; anything you do not want to use your best brushes for.

Paint brushes themselves are typically made from either synthetic weave or natural hair. Synthetic brushes don't tend to hold paint as well as natural brushes; however, when working with acrylic paint this isn't too much of a hindrance as you will be cleaning the brush anyway thanks to the rapid drying times of the paint. Natural brushes do tend to give you better control over the application of paint. Natural brushes are better at retaining their point for precision application, and also hold more paint, giving the added benefit of being able to keep working on a subject for longer. Natural fibre bristles are at their best when used for detail work, especially painting areas such as faces or fine layered highlights.

As you work, you will naturally need to clean your brush. When using most acrylic paints, a simple pot of water will be sufficient for use between changing colours and to prevent paint drying in the bristles. Regardless of what your brush's bristles are made from, I'd not recommend leaving it any longer than a few minutes between giving it a quick swish around in some water. You can add a little washing-up liquid to your water too, though I've not found it necessary myself.

For more long-term care, there are a wide range of brush cleaners and conditioners on the market, and frequently there are products put out from each of the major paint ranges. It's worth investing in either some brush cleaner or, better yet, some brush soap to prevent excess wear or damage to your brushes' bristles. Odourless brush cleaner can be especially handy for aiding restoring brushes. Each of these products will have their own set of specific instructions, usually printed on the side of the packaging, but typically involve giving the brush a solid swishing around in the cleaner/soap, leaving it to stand for a bit and then rinsing

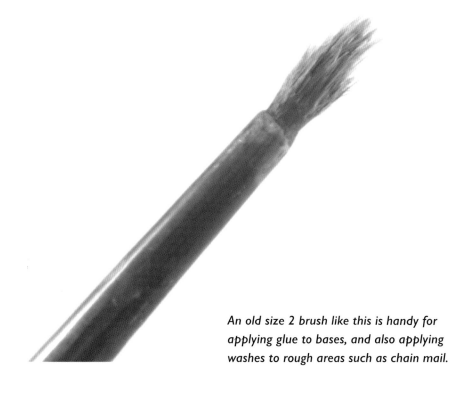

An old size 2 brush like this is handy for applying glue to bases, and also applying washes to rough areas such as chain mail.

clean and shaping. I've used a combination of brush soap and high-end sable brushes to keep the same fine brushes in use nearly every day for four years now!

With regards to what size and shape brush you should be getting, a size 0, a size 1 and a size 2 round should be sufficient. Though it may seem counterintuitive, a brush with a good quality point and fairly long bristles will be far more useful and give a much better result than a tiny size 000 for the vast majority of painting work.

You'll probably spot in the painting guides the use of flat brushes, and these are just what they sound like: a flat, chisel-like brush. These are great for dry brushing as they have a good amount of control, and lend themselves well to pulling over the raised detail, allowing you to have fairly precise highlights quickly. They aren't compulsory for dry brushing, but do make life a lot easier.

A size ½ flat brush for dry brushing.

PAINTING TECHNIQUES

Over the course of the painting guides, I'll be referring to several techniques. Rather than repeat myself in each guide, I'll cover a few of the basic ones here, and then they are ready for you to add to your toolbox.

DRY BRUSHING

Dry brushing is, as the name implies, the technique of using a small amount of paint on a dry brush, to build up layers of colour by quickly flicking the brush over the surface of the model. This will have the effect of adding a contrasting colour to raised areas, whilst leaving the remaining parts of the figure in shade.

Whilst simple in concept, it can take a little practice to really become proficient with dry brushing. Foremost, one must endeavour to keep the brush you are using as dry as possible. Once your paints are applied to the

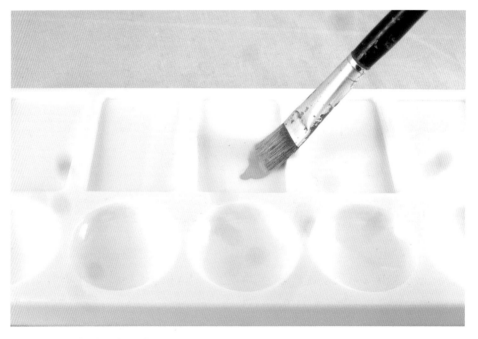

Loading the dry brush with paint.

Removing paint from the brush.

Applying the dry brush.

pallet, avoid thinning them and just load up the tip of the brush with a tiny amount of paint. Clean this paint from the brush with some tissues, then test to see how much paint is present by lightly dragging the bristles over some card or an old figure. You want the paint to be landing on the tops of creases, folds and details of the model, but also want to avoid streaking or blobbing of paint. With dry brushing it's best to allow several layers of paint to build up to achieve the effect you are aiming for, as opposed to going in with one initial, heavy dry brush which can overwhelm your model.

LAYERING

Layering (and edge highlighting) is a somewhat labour-intensive way to add highlights and shade to your figures, and essentially is simply the process of painting in contrasting colours to create the illusion of depth and shade. You'll need to thin your paint a little more than you would usually; it's hard to give a precise mix of ratios, but by eyeballing it you want something fairly thin, but that equally won't flood the model. You need enough paint on the brush for the paint to flow smoothly from the brush, though not so much that it spills and floods once you apply it to the figure surface. You'll be applying the paint to anywhere on the model that catches the light, such as edges of creases, hems of garments, tips of cheeks and noses, etc. To get the

Adding paint to a palette.

most natural look, pick a direction for the light to be directed from, and use this to guide where your highlights or shadows land.

For more eye-catching highlights, keep applying increasing amounts of ever lighter highlights to the model, applying the highlight to only the highest, most prominent areas of detail.

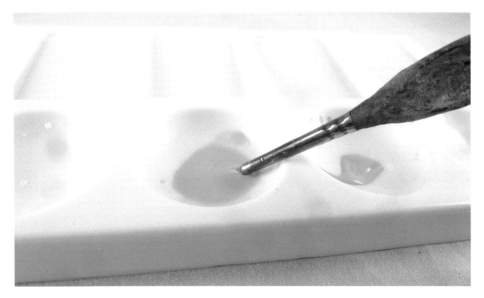

Thinning the paint.

Using a size 2 round brush to apply a highlight.

WASHING AND GLAZING

A wash is a heavily thinned paint applied to a model that flows and settles in the details of the model. These can be purchased as ready-mixed forms, or you can make your own. To make your own, simply add two to three parts of water, with a little washing-up liquid or flow improver, to one part paint, and then mix these together. Paint this solution over the figure, and allow this to accumulate in recesses and details, whilst trying not to allow the wash to pool. This can be caused by too much wash being applied, thus flooding the model. A wash is best applied with an older, though still well-shaped brush, with soft bristles.

A glaze is a similar technique to a wash, and is used to unify the highlights and shades already applied. The process is largely the same as applying a wash, yet is applied far more sparingly. For applying a glaze, simply use a less heavily loaded brush than you would a wash, and paint this over the

Applying a thin glaze over the tunic.

model allowing the colour of the glaze to form on the figure, but without flowing into the recesses as heavily as a wash would. This is a very subtle technique, and is likely to be one of the last you apply to a figure.

VARNISH

A varnish is a clear protective layer applied to the model to protect the paint finish during handling. Gloss varnishes are highly shiny, but they are also very hard-wearing. Naturally, being shiny is not overly realistic for our desert fighting models, so this brings in the use of a matt or flat varnish instead. Whether you use just one type of varnish, both types or none at all is entirely up to you. Typically I choose not to varnish as it can have the effect of dulling the paint (plus I don't get to game with my models that often). However, if you're anticipating heavy use and handing, varnish is pretty much required.

Varnishes can be obtained in many forms, but most useful for our purposes are those in spray cans. Spray cans allow you to varnish many figures quickly and evenly, and have the added bonus of generally being touch dry reasonably quickly. Avoid spraying on hot or humid days, however, as this can cause the paint to cloud and potentially ruin your paint job! Brush-applied varnish will give you more control, and is far less likely to cloud or have some adverse, weather-related failing on your lovingly finished figure!

Hopefully these tips and techniques will have you feeling confident about getting on with assembling and painting your figures, and as ever should be treated as a stepping-off point for your own experiments. Now on to actually building your models.

BOOT CAMP (*CALIGAE CASTRUM?*)

So, with our tools collected and our miniatures sat on the desk, it's time to start getting them ready for paint. With multipart figures becoming increasingly commonplace, it's probably a good idea to cover the best, most stress-free way to assemble your figures.

Whilst we've already covered tools pretty thoroughly, and this should be all the tools you need, it's probably worth getting hold of some fine grade wet and dry sandpaper for cleaning up awkward shapes or particularly fine and light mould lines that may be too fine to require attacking with a file, especially when working with plastic figures.

Whilst metal figures are usually single-piece models, or at most a separate head or limb, plastic figures, especially those in 28mm size, are frequently provided in multiple components, especially cavalry or heavily equipped infantry. This can be surprisingly time-consuming and labour intense, and there is an inherent amount of potential frustration in working with so many components.

There are several steps for alleviating this, however. First of all, take the time to plan what you actually intend the figure to be used for. Will it be an individual figure? Will it be an officer as part of a command diorama, or will it be part of a regiment of warriors on a shared base? This will help you plan out the rest of the assembly process, as it will guide you in visualizing the finished display. I highly recommend working in batches for this process too; my preference is to work in full units (though perhaps not when I get around to doing a barbarian horde), however, batches of five to ten figures is generally popular, without being too daunting.

Batches of this size mean that you can complete gluing a set of parts to one figure, and then work through the group. By the time you are finished with the last, the first should be dry enough for you to do the next stage of assembly with. I also recommend using these batches when painting too, as by the time you've painted the last figure in the group, the first should be dry enough for the next layer. More on this later.

Now that you know how many figures you need, firstly remove their bodies and, if separate, legs from the sprues, clean up any mould lines and stick these onto the model bases. If you are using MDF or resin bases you'll need to superglue the models to those bases.

We're now ready to start adding our figures' arms. When building Romans, you'll often have to choose between *pila* and *gladius*; it's typically better to pick one weapon type for all of the models in one of your units.

I'd recommend leaving the shields off the model for now, adding them after painting is completed.

When posing your figures, take a bit of time dry-fitting and playing around with the arms and bodies to see what sort of poses they create, as some can work considerably better than others. A static figure with a thrusting sword, won't work particularly well; however, the same arm on a set of striding forwards legs will work far better.

Some figures may have separate spears or other weapons. These can require drilling through the hand with a pin vice. It's easier to drill through the hand at either end, rather than simply attempting to drill through the hand from one end.

Now the arms are on, it's simply a matter of attaching the head. Again, it's worth test-fitting the parts first, as sometimes the neck may need a little trimming at the base to ensure the best possible fit. Although an easy task, the position of the head is pretty critical to the final appearance of the figure.

The head and face are pretty much always the focal point of a model, and as such need to be positioned in a way that is complimentary to the rest of the model. The aforementioned figure striding forwards wielding his *gladius* will appear far more threatening glaring forwards; his head positioned looking over his shoulder will have him instead appear to be casting an eye along the battle line and checking his position.

The beauty of plastic models is that the amount of poses and armament combinations possible from even a single box is simply staggering. The sheer variety of poses, however, is daunting, and I can't recommend highly enough trying out some of the poses for yourself to see if they actually work and feel 'right', as it's all too easy coming up with something that looks spectacular, until you find an arm can't actually bend that way, or there's now no room for the head to fit without some spectacular neck problems!

PAINTING GUIDES

Now that the figures are built, we can move on to painting them. Throughout these guides I'll be working over a black primer, as this gives a richer base to work up from, and is also easier for working on the figures in batches.

The bulk of these guides are aimed at providing the start of some ideas on colours and techniques you can use for painting your legions, and should be treated as a stepping-off point, rather than prescribed text. Feel free to replace paints with your preferred ranges and colours.

Throughout these guides I've used 28mm figures, predominantly from Warlord Games, though also some Victrix and Wargames Foundry. They are all either metal or plastic.

I have decided against producing individual guides for legionaries, auxilia, cavalry, etc, as the amount of crossover in equipment renders this impractical. Instead, the guides are broken down by area. I'll tackle armour, shields, flesh, horses and tunics each in their own chapters, before finishing off with some tips on basing your figures. As you read through the guides, you'll notice that a lot of them use the same washes and shades through each step. By combining several of these techniques as you work through a batch, you can get a solid pile of figures done quickly.

Early Imperial
Roman Weapons and Armour

By the end of the first century AD, the Roman legionary had evolved into possibly the most recognizable fighting man of all time. The legionary wears articulated, segmented plate armour, *lorica segmentata*, and on his head is the crested Imperial Gallic helmet with cheek and neck protection. The legionary carries a large rectangular shield, the *scutum*, for further protection. Offensively, he wields both the short stabbing *gladius* sword and *pugio* knife, and caries a pair of *pilum* throwing spears.

Whilst this image is broadly speaking a solid representation of the legionary, the segmented armour was but one of four types of body armour used by the Roman military in the Early Imperial period, the others being *lorica hamata*, *lorica squamata* and *lorica musculata*.

Perhaps the oldest pattern of metal body armour recorded is metal scale armour. As with so many things, the armour probably found its way into Roman use through the Mediterranean, with the earliest recorded scale armour appearing in Egypt during the reign of Amenhotep II. Despite the antiquity of design, scale armour remained in service throughout the entire Roman period and beyond, to the point where at least one modern manufacturer of body armour today still follows the principles of the armour's construction.

Following the reforms of Marius in 107 BC, the Roman legion dispensed with the numerous classes of soldier of the Republican legion, and adopted the armament of the *principes*, a heavily armed and armoured class of soldier.

The primary weapon of the Roman legionary was the *gladius*. This is a short, stabbing sword, with a blade roughly between 45 to 70cm. Cavalry were equipped with a similar, though longer *spatha* sword. Constructed with a steel blade and either wood, bone or bronze hilt, the weapon was designed for close order combat against opposing infantry, with the shield used to block blows and the sword thrusting into an opponent, as opposed to having a secondary, defensive parrying role.

Before using their *gladius*, however, the legionary would be throwing his *pilum*. Whilst this may at first glance appear to be a spear, it was in actuality a throwing javelin though it could be used as a spear if the situation demanded it, such as when fighting a cavalry opponent. The *pilum* features a long, metal shaft behind an armour-piercing point. This was attached to a long, heavy wooden shaft, the weight of which would help to propel the *pilum* into the unfortunate target. Auxilia acting as infantry, as well as cavalry, would be equipped with a more traditional javelin, that again could be used as a thrusting spear.

In Roman use, scale armour is known as *lorica squamata*. It would be constructed from iron, steel, bronze or copper alloy plates, arrayed as the scales of a fish and bound together with wire, and attached to a (most likely) leather layer of vest, and featured a double layer of protection at the shoulder and chest. *Lorica squamata* extended to a similar thigh length as the *lorica hamata*, though offered considerably more protection.

Lorica squamata provided a very thorough level of protection. The combination of scales and leather served to not only prevent penetration injuries, but also to dissipate the kinetic energy of a strike. Mail armour is probably the most persistent and common armour design within the Roman military, and does appear to be worn by all ranks, for infantry, cavalry and auxilia. The armour is heavy, though allows a good range of mobility, but is also expensive and time-consuming to manufacture. The armour is capable of sustaining fairly extensive wear and damage whilst retaining full protection, and in the case of extensive damage the plates are simple to remove and replace quickly if needed.

The optio here is inspecting a group of **lorica segmentata-***clad legionaries.*

Lorica hamata was adopted by the Romans from Celtic mail armour patterns, first appearing around 300 BC in Roman use after being encountered in Cisalpine Gaul. The armour continuing to be equipped until the end of the Empire.

Consisting of a thigh-length mail shirt with a second layer of mail at the shoulder to provide extra protection from any downward strikes, the mail armour was constructed from iron rings, either riveted or butted together. *Lorica hamata* was worn fairly loose fitting over the soldiers' tunic, the weight being distributed by the legionaries' straps and belts. Whilst the protection offered was very good and allowed a good range of mobility, the armour was very time-consuming and expensive to make, and heavy to wear. Fortunately, it was relatively easy to care for and maintain.

A Scorpio crew. One wears **lorica segmentata,** *whilst the other crew member wears* **lorica hamata.**

The iconic *lorica segmentata* first appears around 9 BC but doesn't become prevalent until the latter half of the first century AD. Typically constructed from around forty interlinked steel or iron plates held together via a leather framework, the armour provided superb mobility and protection to the torso and shoulders, and extended to around the waist. Fittings would typically be brass or a copper alloy. The origins of segmented armour are uncertain, and it may be one of the few types of armour whose design was organic to Rome.

The armour was constructed from sheet metal and well suited to both mass production and serviceability in the field, so is the ideal armour for a large field army. *Lorica segmentata* offered similar levels of protection to the *lorica squamata*, but was easier and cheaper to produce. Despite this, the armour offered the legionary good levels of protection against any threat he may encounter on the battlefield.

*Legionaries wearing **lorica segmentata** breach a fortress gate. Several of them are also wearing **manica** arm protection.*

The muscled cuirass, the *lorica musculata*, as made popular in movies from the 1960s and fancy dress costumes, creates a popular image of a high-status Roman, though would be less common in the Early Imperial period. Originating in classic Greece, the armour made its way into Italy and was worn until the introduction of *lorica hamata*. The *lorica musculata* didn't disappear from use, however, and still appears in frescos and statues throughout the *Principate* period. The muscle cuirass appears to have been used by senior officers, and is also worn by statues of numerous emperors, notably Augustus.

Lorica musculata would typically feature leather fringes at both the shoulder and waist, to protect those areas not covered by the cuirass. The cuirass could be made from bronze, iron, steel, copper alloy or leather, and would frequently feature a stylized muscular male torso, with additional religious iconography providing some detail. Whilst leather fringes could be attached to the legionaries' shoulder armour, providing some protection to the upper arm, additional protection to the arm

A pair of officers wearing **lorica musculata** *muscle cuirasses.*

could be worn. Constructed in a similar segmented fashion to the *lorica segmentata, manica* was most likely adopted from arm protection used by several classes of gladiator, notably the heavily armoured *crupellarii* and the *secutor*. Although typically associated with use during Trajan's Dacian Wars, where the sickle-like Dacian *falx* was capable of devastating injuries, archaeological evidence of the armour has been discovered across much of the Empire.

Whilst much of the legionary's body was protected by his *scutum* (shield), this did leave his shins somewhat exposed. Like the muscle cuirass, the Romans adopted greaves, or *ocrea*, from the Greeks to protect the lower leg. Greaves were simple to produce and could be made from a range of metals, though would most likely be iron or copper alloy for the average legionary.

The helmet adopted by the Roman military is both distinctive and iconic, but also not Roman.

By the period we're modelling, the Imperial Gallic helmet had become prevalent; however, its design is rooted in a Celtic-designed helmet. This was a simple, bowl-shaped helmet with a small neck guard. To this design the Romans added cheek guards, with the helmet then evolving to have a larger neck guard, extra protective banding, decoration and detail work.

At its core, the Gallic helmet provided excellent situational awareness, with good vision and hearing, balanced against solid protection whilst remaining wearable and practical. Fittings could typically be brass or bronze, although at least one example has been recovered from Germany with fittings enamelled red.

Whilst iron was the most common material for helmet production, copper alloy and even bronze examples were also used. These helmets appear to be contemporaries to one another, and whether the material they were constructed from was significant to their being issued to infantry, cavalry or auxilia is currently unknown.

Military headgear has long had a wider use than simple head protection, with crests and plumes added to the helmets of the ancient world to increase the intimidation and stature of the wearer, as well as aid in battlefield recognition. The Romans followed this time-honoured trend, with several patterns and forms of crest being worn, most commonly with a crest running from front to rear of the helmet for legionaries, whilst Vegetius records that centurions wore transverse crests. Crests would be made from horsehair. There isn't much knowledge of the colours of the crests, though red, black, purple and white seem the most likely.

The big issue for us as gamers, painters and collectors is how this panoply would have looked in person. In contemporary art, copper and bronze armour are represented in yellow, whilst iron is portrayed with white. Despite being constructed predominantly from iron, the armour would generally have been kept very clean and polished, despite the ease with which iron rusts. Numerous contemporary primary sources refer to gleaming armour and the virtues of smart, clean troops. Notable for us is the work of Onasander, writing in the first century AD:

> For the advancing companies appear more dangerous by the gleam of weapons, and the terrible sight brings fear and confusion to the hearts of the enemy.

Polished iron has a silver appearance, though it does rust and tarnish if not cared for properly and frequently cleaned and maintained. What the Romans used to protect their armour is unknown, though olive oil or bitumen are possible. It is possible that armour could have been blued or blackened as part of the forging process too, though there is no evidence for this being done.

Several examples of tinned helmets have survived and this may well have been applied to other armour, especially greaves. Tinning was a way of protecting iron by applying a coating of tin to the armour as a preservative layer. This gives the armour a bright, gleaming silver finish. Silvering and gilding also occurred, and have been observed on what is most likely ceremonial armour.

The copper alloy also commonly used in Roman armour production has the colour of dull brass and, like bronze armour, can be polished to a golden finish.

From this we can infer that the legionary would have generally appeared clean and well-presented, with polished armour, yet it's probably reasonable to assume a level of tarnish and wear occurring in particularly bad weather, at least on a hard-pressed campaign in the field operating away from the legion's base.

PAINTING ROMAN ARMS AND ARMOUR

Over the next few pages, I'll attempt to illustrate a few different techniques and colour combinations to give a fairly broad range of finishes and appearances to your figures. Please don't feel constrained into just using the paints and colours I suggest, and instead use them as a starting point for your own experiments. All of these figures will be using a black primed base. Whilst you can get metallic sprays, I find they don't save a great deal of time, as getting the colours for the rest of the figure is harder than simply painting each part of the figure individually.

IRON AND STEEL

Lorica hamata

CLEAN IRON MAIL

First of all, we'll try a fairly dark but clean suit of mail. This could be the look for old, well-maintained armour that hasn't been allowed to rust. Once the black primer is dry, we're ready to go straight into painting.

Step 1

To start off, we'll dry brush the model with a dark silver paint, allowing the black in the centre of the rings to show through. If your primer has left parts of the model's material exposed, you may need to paint the model black first with your chosen brand of paint. Ensure you dry brush over as much of the armour as you can.

Brush Used	Paint
Size 2 (or 4) angled brush	Vallejo 863 Gunmetal

Step 2

In this step, we'll add a highlight, to add a bit more vibrancy to the armour. If you want your mail to look bright and polished, you can leave the armour as it is, and go on to paint the rest of the figure. Here, we'll dry brush a brighter silver, allowing the dry brushing to concentrate on the upper areas of the figure that naturally catch the light, such as the tops of shoulders and edges of the mail shirt.

Brush Used	Paint
Size 2 (or 4) angled brush	Vallejo Game Color 053 Chainmail

Step 3

This stage is entirely optional. If you want your armour to look bright and clean, you can skip this step, or you may like to experiment using some of the other washes used with the segmented armour in guides later in this section. However, if you want your armour to appear clean, though used, you can give it a black wash to dull the shine of the metals that are on the mail vest.

When applying your wash, you want the paint to flow into the detail, but not flood it either, so try not to overload your brush too much, and ensure the paint is smoothly and evenly applied.

Brush Used	Paint
Size 2 round brush	Army Painter Dark Tone

TARNISHED IRON MAIL

To give a worn, hard-campaigning, maybe even winter look to your figures, where time and weather may not be on their side for keeping armour clean and smart, we can use the following to give a darker, more beaten look to the *lorica hamata*.

Step 1
As with the previous guide, we'll start with a black base, and then dry brush our base colour, this time bronze. This will give a warmer, browner tone to the subsequent layers.

Brush Used	Paint
Size 2 (or 4) angled brush	Vallejo Game Color 60 Tinny Tin

Step 2

For the highlight stage, instead of going for the brighter, chainmail colour, we will instead use gunmetal. This will help to keep the darker, duller tone we are trying to achieve for this armour.

Brush Used	Paint
Size 2 (or 4) angled brush	Vallejo 863 Gunmetal

Step 3

You can now decide to leave the model as it is or add a wash of a dark brown colour. This will greatly enhance the grimy appearance of the armour, and make your figure appear as if he has been involved in some hard campaigning.

Brush Used	Paint
Size 2 round brush	Army Painter Strong Tone

Step 4

If you decide you don't want your figures to look quite so muted or dirty, you can bring the metallic shine back up, with another dry

brush of gunmetal. If you want to really vary the appearance of the figures in a unit, you can paint the figures to various steps of these guides, so some may be up to step 2, some step 3 and others step 4. This will serve to add a bit of variety, but still keep a coherent-looking unit.

Brush Used	Paint
Size 2 (or 4) angled brush	Vallejo 863 Gunmetal

LORICA SEGMENTATA

As we've seen, *lorica segmentata* is typically constructed from iron or steel, and well-maintained. For painting segmented armour, we'll do two clean and well-maintained suits, and one with a more worn, weathered appearance. To help emphasize the clean sharp edges, we'll be using the edge highlight technique for two of the guides. These guides can also be used for painting iron and steel helmets. For the brass fittings on the armour, we'll cover those with the other items of brass and bronze armour.

CLEAN SEGMENTATA

First off, let's do a smart legionary with some fresh, well-maintained armour. We're aiming for a clean, bright metal, so will be using selective washes and some neat edge highlighting.

In step 1, we're going to just give a neat, tidy coat of gunmetal over the armour. It's better to use two thinner coats, rather than one thick coat of paint.

Step 1

Brush Used	Paint
Size 2 round brush	Vallejo 863 Gunmetal

Step 2

To shade the plates in the segments of the armour, we'll apply a dark wash just to the gaps of the armour. Try to be as neat as you can, and allow capillary action to aid the flow of the wash into the detail. Try to

avoid letting the wash flow onto the rest of the armour, although if it does, it doesn't matter too much, as we can tidy the armour up when we do the highlights.

Brush Used	Paint
Size 2 round brush	Army Painter Dark Tone

Step 3

Edge highlighting the armour will serve to make the armour appear brighter and crisper. If you're not comfortable with painting the edges, or you want to get through painting a batch of figures quicker, you can use the dry brush technique instead.

Brush Used	Paint
Size 1 round brush (or Size 2 angled brush for dry brushing)	Vallejo Game Color 053 Chainmail

AGED *SEGMENTATA*

Whilst well-maintained, natural use and exposure to the elements would serve to add at least some darkening and change in colour to the plates of segmented armour, and have it appear less bright and gleaming than a freshly polished suit.

Step 1

To get an older, darker though still well-maintained suit of segmented armour, we'll be using the same paints as for the clean effect, although applying them in a different order. As before, you're free to substitute the edge highlights for dry brushing instead. The first stage is to paint the model's armour with gunmetal; again, for a solid, even finish you may require two thinner coats of paint.

Brush Used	Paint
Size 2 round brush	Vallejo 863 Gunmetal

Step 2

Now, instead of applying the highlight after the wash, we'll highlight the armour now. This is to add a highlight to the plates and stop the armour appearing to be too bright and shiny. It will serve to distinguish it from the cleaner stage. You can opt to dry brush or layer the paint on; I've opted to layer it on here.

Brush Used	Paint
Size 1 round brush (or Size 2 angled brush for dry brushing)	Vallejo Game Color 053 Chainmail

Step 3

Creating a dull steel or iron effect quickly is very easy to do: simply apply a black wash all over the armour. You can also experiment with other

colour washes. Browns would give a light rust patina effect, whilst a blue wash gives a cleaner, less tarnished effect.

Brush Used	Paint
Size 2 round brush	Army Painter Dark Tone

Step 4

This is an optional highlight stage, and will alter the surface appearance of the armour to give a greater degree of vibrancy. With the highlights here, whilst you could probably dry brush them, edge highlights will be more appropriate for the appearance we're attempting to achieve. The highlights should be applied sparingly. Paint them onto the lightest edges, on the corners of the shoulder armour and the edges of the torso armour plates. We're going to use smaller, fewer highlights than with step 3 of the clean *segmentata*. For this figure, I've just applied a very light dry brush.

Brush Used	Paint
Size 1 round brush (or Size 2 angled brush for dry brushing)	Vallejo Game Color 053 Chainmail

WEATHERED *SEGMENTATA*

This finish is intended to represent very battered and heavily campaigned in armour. It's hard to say how often the armour may have appeared in this condition, though it does give a strong, narrative feel to an army, even if it might not be historically representative.

Step 1

For this, we'll be using some very similar techniques to the aged *segmentata*, as well as the tarnished mail. We'll start, instead of using gunmetal, with a dry brush of a dark bronze instead, again to give an aged, rusted appearance.

Brush Used	Paint
Size 2 (or 4) angled brush	Vallejo Game Color 60 Tinny Tin

Step 2

We'll dry brush the figure with gunmetal now. This serves to bring in a dull iron colour. You can choose to layer the gunmetal on, but dry brushing gives more of a texture to the armour and leaves the impression of a subtly rougher surface.

Brush Used	Paint
Size 2 (or 4) angled brush	Vallejo 863 Gunmetal

Step 3

To bring back the brown, surface rust, effect we've been building up on the figure's armour, we'll give the armour a layer all over of dark brown wash.

Brush Used	Paint
Size 2 round brush	Army Painter Strong Tone

Step 4

As with the aged armour, if you want to tone down the weathering, and make it appear better maintained and cared for, you can come back and add an edge highlight of gunmetal. You could use a brighter silver, but that would dilute the weathering effect and make the armour appear brighter and cleaner than we've been aiming for. It's worth experimenting on your own figures to see what aesthetic appeals to you.

Brush Used	Paint
Size 1 round brush	Vallejo 863 Gunmetal

BRIGHT BRONZE OR COPPER ALLOY ARMOUR

Well-polished bronze or copper alloy armour has a very striking appearance, being a bold golden colour, and is portrayed as such in contemporary Roman art. To replicate this, we'll use some shiny, bright metallic paints, and build up the colour using layers. This can be used for the armour, helmet and other fittings of figures wearing iron armour, helmets and *lorica squamata* or *musculata*.

Step 1

We're going to start with a layer of bronze over all of the armour. We're trying to achieve smooth, solid colour, so a couple of thin coats will serve better than a single heavy layer.

Brush Used	Paint
Size 2 round brush	Vallejo Game Color 60 Tinny Tin

Step 2

For the first highlight layer, we could dry brush the brass onto the figure; however, we're aiming for a very smooth appearance to the armour. For

this we'll be using layered highlights, allowing the previous bronze colour to show through in the recesses and shade.

Brush Used	Paint
Size 1 round brush	Vallejo Game Color 058 Brassy Brass

Step 3

For this highlight, we will again use edge highlighting, and will be applying the gold paint to the most extreme edges of the armour. If you're painting things like armour fittings on segmented armour, or helmet details, you can choose to skip this step. Alternatively, you may opt to skip step 2 and go straight to a brighter highlight.

Brush Used	Paint
Size 1 round brush	Vallejo Game Color 055 Polished Gold

WEATHERED BRONZE/COPPER ALLOY

When aged, the copper alloy takes on a dull, muted tone and loses its lustrous, golden appearance, becoming quite matt. This is very easy to replicate quickly, and there are a few different appearances we can create.

Step 1

First up, we'll paint the armour brass, as ever using several thin coats if necessary to build up a solid, neat base to work from.

Brush Used	Paint
Size 1 round brush	Vallejo Game Color 058 Brassy Brass

Step 2

Now, to simply dull the armour done, we can use a selection of washes to provide a muted, shaded finish. I've picked several Army Painter washes: Flesh Tone, Soft Tone and Military Shader. Each of these has a different property.

Military Shader will provide a green tint to the brass, and that in turn will make the armour appear older and more heavily worn. Flesh Tone will give the opposite, and instead give it a warmer, less aged appearance, though still dulled down. For somewhere in the middle, you can use Army Painter Soft Tone. This will give a neutral, dull finish to the brass.

Brush Used	Paint
Size 2 round brush	Army Painter Soft Tone, Flesh Tone or Military Shader

BLACKENED ARMOUR

This armour colouring is completely hypothetical, with no evidence to suggest it existed, yet it can give a great effect on models wearing ceremonial segmented or muscular armour, such as officers or guard units. Given the high-status appearance we are aiming to create with this armour, it pairs well with the tinned armour and the bright brass effects we are also covering. I've gone for a dark, subtle appearance to the black, but if you wanted a greater contrast, you could add a very final highlight of gunmetal at the end, concentrating on the most prominent areas. I prefer to keep it simple though, as the other colours of the figure already make it busy and add lots of contrast and interest.

Step 1
We will begin by giving the armour a layer of metallic black paint. As this is being applied over black primer, you should only require one layer, but feel free to do two if necessary.

Brush Used	Paint
Size 2 round brush	Vallejo Model Air 073 Metallic Black

Step 2

To give the armour a more lustrous, polished appearance. Give it a layer all over of a blue wash. This will serve to add a very subtle shift in tone to the colour, and make it appear far richer.

Brush Used	Paint
Size 2 round brush	Army Painter Blue Tone ink

Step 3

This is a final edge highlight of the metallic black once again, to bring up the shine in the armour. Don't worry too much about a lack of contrast between the shadowed areas of the figure, as the contrast with the rest of the colours on the model, such as its tunic and armour details, will make the model visually very striking.

Brush Used	Paint
Size 1 round brush	Vallejo Model Air 073 Metallic Black

TINNED ARMOUR

Tinning was a preservative method applied predominantly to helmets, greaves and occasionally shield bosses and helmet face masks. The effect has the added bonus of giving the item a very bright, shiny silvered finish. Here, we'll give a legionary a tinned helmet, though the effect is also good for metal fittings on scabbards, the medallions on officers and standards, and cavalry face masks.

Step 1

To recreate this effect is very simple. We'll start by painting the armour with a bright silver. As this is a fairly light colour, it will probably require at least two coats, maybe three. However, as the areas being painted are fairly small typically, this isn't too time-consuming.

Brush Used	Paint
Size 2 round brush	Army Painter Plate Mail

Step 2

Instead of using a black or brown wash, we'll use a blue to add emphasis to details. Instead of covering the tinned item, simply paint the wash into the recesses and around the details, being careful to prevent the wash from flooding or pooling.

Brush Used	Paint
Size 2 round brush	Army Painter Blue Tone ink

Step 3

To finish the armour, and add an extra level of sheen to the piece, apply some layered highlights to the upper surfaces and details, using a very bright silver.

Brush Used	Paint
Size 1 round brush (or Size 2 angled brush for dry brushing)	Vallejo Game Color 053 Chainmail

WOOD FITTINGS

Whilst not metal, this seems the most appropriate place to put a few ideas for adding some ideas on painting the wood fittings on weapons, as well as on artillery pieces. You have quite a bit of room for interpretation with the wooden items, and can choose to treat them as painted wood if you so wish. Here though, we'll go for a dark wood effect.

On the Roman legionary, the haft of the *pilum*, spear shafts, *gladius* grips and framework of artillery would all be constructed from wood (though the grip could be other materials, and appearances, such as brass or ivory, depending on the status of the soldier).

Step 1

We'll be painting this legionary's *pilum*, however, all of these techniques can apply to any of the already listed areas. All of the metal parts of the *pilum* have already been painted using the same techniques as on the legionary's armour.

We'll go for a deep, rich brown here, with the aim of being fairly subtle to avoid drawing attention from the rest of the figure. Simply paint the areas with your chosen base colour, being careful not to get any paint on the areas of the model already painted.

Brush Used	Paint
Size 2 round brush	Vallejo 822 German Camouflage Black Brown

Step 2

Here we'll add a highlight layer to the weapon. It's entirely down to personal taste how much you want to do here, and you can even simply skip this stage if you so wish. I'm going to be quite sparing with the highlight, and only add them to the sharpest edges and places most likely to catch the light.

Brush Used	Paint
Size 1 round brush	Vallejo 940 Saddle Brown

Step 3

To enhance the richness of the wood effect, we'll apply a purple shader all over the wooden areas. If you're aiming for a fresh, untreated wood effect, then the Army Painter camo shader can work very well over pale browns.

Brush Used	Paint
Size 2 round brush	Army Painter Purple Tone ink

Shields

The large rectangular shield, the *scutum*, carried by the Roman legionary by the beginning of the Early Imperial period is a hugely distinctive part of the Roman panoply, but there were other shapes in use too. Prior to the adoption of the rectangular shield, the legionary had carried an oval shield, and this persisted in use with auxilia and cavalry units. Smaller round shields also appeared, carried by standard bearers and musicians predominantly.

The traditional rectangular *scutum* was constructed from three alternating layers of wooden strips, glued together, then sealed with a covering, possibly linen or leather. To further reinforce the shield, a metal edging strip was added, being simply nailed through the wood to attach it. In the centre of the shield is a thick metal boss. The shield is held by a grip running left to right across the centre of the shield, protected by the shield boss. There is no strap to the shield when used for fighting.

The *scutum* could be used both offensively and defensively. While attacking, the legionary could punch the mass and weight of the shield at an opponent to drive them back and unbalance them. The metal edging further allowed him to use the shield offensively by driving the edge up and into an opponent's face and neck.

Of course the main use of the shield was defensive. The alternating layers of wood gave a great deal of flexibility and strength to the shield, and the heft of the boss rendered the bearer's hand impervious to all but the most potent of strikes. Individually, the protection was very good, but the legionary did not fight alone and was able to present his shield as part of an intimidating wall to his enemy.

The rectangular shape rendered the creation of complex formations possible, such as the famous *testudo*, where the legionaries would be protected from all angles and be able to advance on a fortified position in relative safety.

Offensively, the century would form into a wedge and assault their opponents. The combination of heavy armour, the large shields and barrage of *pila* rendered this charge devastating against most opponents, until the arrival of the horse archer on the ancient battlefield.

With regards to actual colours and appearance of the shields, we have very little information, especially for the Early Imperial period. That said, there are a few sources we can pull together to get a few ideas, notably Trajan's Column and the *Notitia Dignitatum*.

Trajan's Column is a 190-metre-long frieze winding around a 30-metre-tall column commemorating the Emperor Trajan's victory over the Dacians in the Dacian Wars. It was constructed only a few years after the wars' end, and features thousands of carved figures, demonstrating a huge array of Roman military hardware. Notable for our purposes is a depiction of a *testudo* formation, with all the shields featuring the same device, the famous wings and lightning bolts, though various other devices are also depicted being carried by other legionaries and auxilia. What this really means we don't know, but it's

not unreasonable to assume each legion or auxilia cohort would have had its own device.

The *Notitia Dignitatum*, or 'list of offices', dates to around the fourth century, so considerably later than our period, but it does still offer some useful information. Crucially, it included a detailed study of Roman shields which gives us a good guide as to the colouration used.

Probably the most prevalent colour for the shield is red, though blue and yellow also occur frequently. Green, black and white shields also occur, though are less common. For the Early Imperial period, this is mostly likely to translate to the front and rear of the shield being one of these colours, with a legion or cohort's specific device then added.

With the shield covering such a significant part of the figure, they become a massively important focal point of the figure. Thankfully, there is a huge range of transfers on the market to aid us with the complex designs found on shields throughout the entire Roman period.

Whilst you can freehand the designs, this is fairly time-consuming and can end up being a great deal of work. It can look spectacular on one-off figures, but it goes a bit beyond the scope of this book. That said, if you do decide to do some of your own shield designs, I suggest a few practice runs on spare parts or card, and sketching out the design in pencil as a guide.

With all these shields, those with riveted edges and shield bosses will be painted using the metal techniques covered in the previous chapters, and will also be painted using a white primer. With them all, I suggest doing the design and colour of the shield first, then coming back and adding in the details.

PLAIN SOLID COLOUR SHIELD

The simplest type of shield we can do, unsurprisingly, is one of a solid single colour with no design or pattern. As we've already seen, shields can come in a range of colours. Here we'll work on a deep red shield destined for a cavalryman. With all of these shields, the rear is painted in the same colours as the front.

Step 1

Over a white primer, we're going to paint on a solid base colour. To get a vibrant colour, this will require two or three thin coats, but if you're working on a batch then by the time you get to the last one, the first should be ready for a second coat.

Brush Used	Paint
Size 2 round brush	Vallejo Game Color 011 Gory Red

Step 2

To add some interest to the shield, we'll apply a highlight to the upper part, aiming to apply the paint thinly to the upper quarter or so, and letting it blend or fade into the main shield colour. For a highlight, you don't want to have too much contrast between base and highlight colour, so for this shield we'll be using a medium red. I'll also pick out the metal parts of the shield, in this case using gunmetal for the shield boss and bronze for the edging of the shield.

Brush Used	Paint
Size 2 round brush	Vallejo 957 Flat Red

Step 3

If you wish, you can add a little shadow to the shield. This is the reverse of the process in step 2, and simply involves adding a shade to the lower half of the shield. To contrast the deep red, we'll use some strong tone shade from the Army Painter, as this will give a weathered, well-used appearance. Alternatively, a green or purple tone could be used to give a brighter, more lustrous finish to the shield.

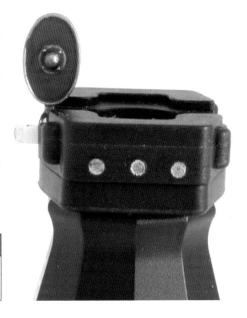

Brush Used	Paint
Size 2 round brush	Army Painter Strong Tone

TRANSPARENT DECAL

So, now that we've covered creating a simple mono colour shield, we can start to bring in some transfers. Some of these feature a design or pattern on a transparent carrier film which is then applied to a previously painted shield.

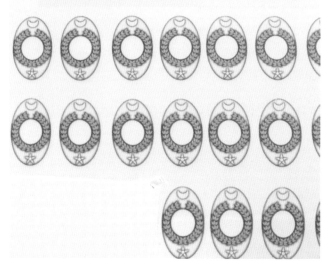

Step 1

Paint a solid base colour onto your shield. Here we're going to work on an auxiliary infantryman's shield, and I've chosen to do this cohort with a bright blue colour. We'll apply this base colour over white to ensure a solid vibrancy.

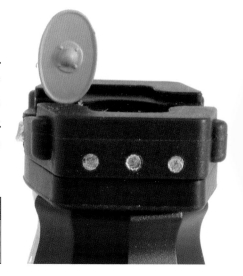

Brush Used	Paint
Size 2 round brush	Vallejo Game Color 024 Magic Blue

Step 2

Before we can apply the decal, it's advisable to paint the area to receive the transfer with some gloss varnish. Primarily, this is to aid with slipping the decal from its backing paper; there is less surface tension than with matt paint, so it becomes easier to move to its final position. It's worth leaving the varnish to dry overnight before going on to the next step

Brush Used	Paint
Size 2 round brush	Vallejo 510 Gloss Varnish

Step 3

Transfers are provided on a sheet of backing paper, usually with many designs on one sheet, and so require a little preparation. With waterslide transfers, these have a carrier film with a printed design. Some sheets are covered in carrier film, and require you to prepare the transfer by carefully cutting around the edge of the design with the sharp blade of your hobby knife.

Luckily, however, the ones I am using here are pre-trimmed and ready to use, and only need roughly cutting out. I tend to use a small pot

of warm water for soaking transfers, then whilst gripping the transfer in some tweezers, dunk it in the pot for a few seconds before lifting it out and letting it sit for a moment.

With an old brush, I'll gently push the transfer to see if it moves freely on the backing paper. If it does, it's able to be applied to the model. Either lift the transfer with the brush, or hold the transfer and its backing paper next to the shield, then slide the design from the paper onto the model.

Once you are happy with the position of the transfer, gently press down with your old brush to drive out any excess water behind the transfer, and leave to dry. Be aware that whilst it is drying, the transfer is very delicate and can lift or be damaged easily.

Step 4

Most decals dry to a gloss finish once they are dried, and you may decide that you want to have a more muted experience. To do so, simply paint a layer of matt varnish over the shield. The decal I've used here has a black edging. However, as this doesn't actually fit the shield I've applied the transfer to, I've also gone back over this area with the base colour and picked out the shield boss in gun metal.

Brush Used	Paint
Size 2 round brush	Vallejo 520 Matt Varnish

Step 5

If you wish to add a little weathering, you can repeat step 3 of the solid colour shield guide, working a darker colour onto the lower part of the shield. Here I've used Strong Tone again, as I'm intending to keep a uniform level of weathering across my whole collection.

If you want to go into more detail on your shields, you can use the solid colour shield guide, and then go on to adding transfers as detailed here. You are now ready to pick out any areas of metal work on the shield.

Brush Used	Paint
Size 2 round brush	Army Painter Strong Tone

SOLID COLOUR DECAL

These are very similar to transparent decals, though instead of being transparent they include a backing colour. This saves us from having to paint the front of the shield, though the rear will still need blocking in to match.

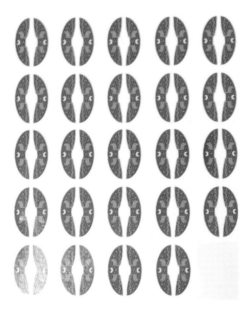

Step 1

As some transfers can be a little lacking in opacity, we will apply them directly over our white base. First of all, we'll apply a gloss varnish and leave this to dry.

Brush Used	Paint
Size 2 round brush	Vallejo 510 Gloss Varnish

Step 2

I've carefully trimmed this Praetorian's shield from the backing sheet, so as to limit any overlap from the carrier film. This will help to make a neater, smarter looking model when painting the metal guttering on the edge of the shield. Other than that, the decal is applied in the same way as already covered.

Step 3

Fairly simple this, we just give the decal a coat of matt varnish once it's dried. This is also a good time to pick out the metal parts of the shield.

Brush Used	Paint
Size 2 round brush	Vallejo 520 Matt Varnish

Step 4

We now paint the back of the shield in a colour as close as we can to the decal on the front of the shield. You may find you need to neaten up around the edges of the shield transfer too if there is any white showing through. As the decal is a fairly deep red, we're going to use an equally dark red. Once this is done, you can finish the shield off with the details of its guttering and shield boss. You can also optionally choose to add weathering using a dark black or brown wash to the shield if you wish.

Brush Used	Paint
Size 2 round brush	Vallejo Game Color 011 Gory Red

There are also a few ideas for bringing your shields to life. You can use off-whites and pale sand colours to paint on scratches and wear to shields if you really want to add some battle damage, and even blood spatters and clotted mud to get the feel of being in the thick of fighting.

When I am working on shields, I tend to do them in fairly big batches, typically all of the shields for a unit in one go, as it can be a fairly tedious, repetitive job, so I like to get it out of the way in one go. I also try to avoid fitting the shields until the very last stage of the model, as they can get in the way whilst trying to base your models, given their size.

5

Tunics, Helmet Crests and Cloaks

Beneath his armour, the Roman legionary and auxiliary wore his tunic. Typically this is a knee-length, sleeveless garment, though sleeves gradually became more commonplace. In colder climates, the legionary slowly adopted trousers, for obvious practical reasons, though it seems cavalry may have been using them for a significantly longer period.

Auxilia are sometimes depicted wearing their native dress, notably a group of archers on Trajan's Column wearing eastern dress of long robes. However, they are more commonly portrayed in a more uniform style of mail, tunic and, where appropriate, trousers, as well as the relevant weaponry for their particular cohort's battlefield role.

The colour of the tunic has been the topic for debate. The bulk of surviving evidence suggests that red and undyed white were the most common. Auxilia probably wore the same as legionaries, although there is at least some evidence of them wearing their native clothing, so there could be some leeway in colour here.

Numerous portraits of soldiers in Egypt all show white tunics, whilst documents from all over the Empire further reinforce this. The tunic itself was wool. Undyed wool can range through yellows, browns and off-white shades. It appears the Romans may have had both undyed and treated woollen tunics, as well as white linen. Several documents, including tablets from the fort at Vindolanda on Hadrian's Wall in northern England, also reference officers having white clothing.

As nothing is ever simple, however, red tunics also appear in some contemporary art and frescos, though the significance is unknown. Isidore of Seville, writing in the early seventh century in his *Etymologiae*, refers to the Roman military in the Republican era wearing red tunics only in battle. It is assumed he was writing using contemporary texts

A pair of legionaries huddling into their cloaks.

that are now lost to us, though it does open up other options to us as hobbyists.

The appearance of the red colour is also open to debate, and seems to range from an orange-brown colour to scarlet, pinkish red and burgundy. Most common through the Roman world, however, is Madder Red: a rich, dark red with an almost purple-pinkish tone to it.

Other colours, notably blue, green and yellow, though also black in the case of one auxiliary unit, do sometimes occur.

Green was expensive to make, and doesn't appear to have been a popular or fashionable choice in the Roman world. That said, a guard of the Emperor Justinian is portrayed wearing green in a mosaic, although this is 400 or so years after our period. It's not impossible for high-status units to have been equipped with some more expensive dyed items of clothing.

Blue is another less frequently seen colour of clothing, though it does appear as a tunic colour in several frescos, notably on several portrayals of cavalrymen. Vegetius notes the men of the *Classis*

A senior officer wearing a purple cloak meets with a native dignitary.

Britannicus, the Roman Navy in Britain, wearing blue. Several portrait paintings from Egypt, identified as centurions, also have men wearing blue cloaks. Interestingly, the cavalry fresco portrays the men wearing red leggings.

Cloaks were a key part of the military wardrobe, being a key identifier of his status as a soldier. Officers, especially centurions, are most commonly seen in surviving evidence as wearing red cloaks, although others, such as the previously mentioned blue, are also noted. Predominantly, the soldier's cloak worn by the legionary is an ochre brown colour, though this seems to vary in shade, and red also appears.

Senior officers in command of a legion would have had the funds and status to wear purple capes, though this becomes an increasingly common colour once cheaper dyes are discovered. These are later than our period though.

Although not always apparent in surviving contemporary presentation of legionaries, horsehair helmet crests do still appear, most commonly on centurions, where they are affixed transversely to the helmet. Other ranks appear to wear their crests front to back.

This auxiliary centurion is ably demonstrating how recognizable his cape and helmet crest are in battle.

Colouration is hard to pin down, though Polybious, writing before the Early Imperial period, notes crests are of red, black and purple. White is also apparently quite common. Arrian, writing in the second century, noted crests of yellow for cavalry. Blue and green do not seem to appear, at least not with any regularity.

Many figures wear scarves and ties at the neck, and there's no real evidence for what colour these might have been, so feel free to pick from those already discussed.

What does all this mean to us as painters? Well, we have a fair amount of flexibility. With legionaries, when aiming to err on the side of historical accuracy, it's best to go for off-white or red tunics, with helmet crests of either red or white, and cloaks of red for centurions and ochre for the rest of the men. Personally, I paint the legionaries of my collection wearing off-white tunics, with officers having deep red tunics and capes.

Auxiliary and elite units can give us a little more flexibility in colours, for example the Justinian guardsman or the blue and red dress cavalryman. Drawing on my own collection, my Praetorian guardsmen

These auxiliary cavalry are wearing blue tunics, with their officers having yellow crests on their helmets. The blue was painted in the same way as the red tunic in this guide, substituting red ink with blue, with the final highlight colour a light blue.

wear brilliant white tunics with black helmet crests, and my auxiliary cavalry have blue tunics. This can serve to add some pleasant dashes of colours to your collection, breaking up the monotony of ranks of legionaries.

Whilst each of the following guides refers to tunics, they can equally be applied to any other garments or crests worn by your figures as you wish.

OFF-WHITE TUNIC

Step 1

Off-white can cover a huge range of colours, from browns to greys, yellows and even tints of green. I tend to favour a greyish brown, so that's what we'll cover here. Feel free to experiment, as it's hard to go wrong really when sticking to this range of colours. I always prefer to do the armour of a figure first, so we'll be using a figure whose armour we've already painted earlier in this book. Start off by neatly going over all the areas of his tunic with your chosen base colour, in this case a pale grey

Brush Used	Paint
Size 2 round brush	Vallejo 986 Deck Tan

Step 2

We'll now do a rough highlight. This doesn't have to be particularly neat, but should be concentrated on any raised areas, edges of creases and anywhere else likely to draw the light

Brush Used	Paint
Size 1 round brush	Vallejo 837 Pale Sand

Step 3

Once the previous stages are dry, we can now shade the tunic. To do this we will apply a glaze of light brown. Here I'm using Army Painter Soft Tone, applying this thinly all over the tunic as if I were applying a layer of

paint. The trick is to not allow the tone to pool or flood any of the detail. If you want a more worn and grimy look, you can use a darker brown, or even black instead, such as Strong Tone or Dark Tone.

Brush Used	Paint
Size 2 round brush	Army Painter Soft Tone

Step 4

This is an optional stage, though I tend to do it as it brings the contrast back into the tunic and serves to make the model 'pop' a little more visually. With the colour used in step 2, go back and add some neat highlighting again to the edges and centres already highlighted, in places where the light naturally catches on the model.

Brush Used	Paint
Size 1 round brush	Vallejo 837 Pale Sand

BRILLIANT LEATHER ARMOUR

As a natural progression from the off-white tunic, it seems appropriate to cover a technique for a clean and smart white. You may want to use this for officers, or even high-status civilians' clothing and cloaks, and also the leather fringes on an officer's armour. I'm using it here to give a subtle distinction between the more rough-and-ready look of my legionaries and a snappier, sharper appearance for my officers. I'll also be painting this officer's leather armoured fringes to create a very distinctive looking figure.

Step 1
To distinguish the officer from the rougher white tunics of the legionaries, we're going to be aiming for a colder set of colours, and will use a pale green, though a pale blue-grey or blue can work nicely too.

Brush Used	Paint
Size 2 round brush	Vallejo 971 Green Grey

Step 2

We'll now add a little shade to the model by selectively applying a dark blue into the darkest recesses. I'm going to use a pre-mixed shade, but if you wanted to play around with contrast and colours by mixing your own wash, then go for it. Whichever option you go for, carefully apply the shadow colour into the deepest recesses and areas of shade on the figure.

Brush Used	Paint
Size 2 round brush	Army Painter Blue Tone.

Step 3

Obviously, our figure is not looking very white at the moment. To rectify this, we'll first use an off-white colour. I'm using ivory, as I like the contrast with the cold tones already on the figure, though you could use a suitably pale grey instead if you prefer. Thin the paint a little more than you do normally for layering, and apply this to all the raised areas. You can even work it into some of the shallower areas of shade. The objective here is to keep the blue in the darkest areas and the pale green in the middle areas.

Brush Used	Paint
Size 2 round brush	Vallejo 918 Ivory

Step 4

To really bring out the white we'll start applying some highlights, using, perhaps unsurprisingly, white. Again, thin this a little more than usual, and apply it to all the brightest high points and areas that will naturally catch the light. You may need to repeat this step a few times to get a really nice, smooth and bold white.

Brush Used	Paint
Size 1 round brush	Vallejo 951 White

RED TUNIC

As this is something you may want to have a lot of in your army, I'll cover a way to get a nice rich red that's fairly close to Madder Red. Whilst this is going to be painted on a tunic, you'll see other examples of this technique used on centurions' cloaks throughout this book. As an aside, if you want to do green, blue, purple or even yellow tunics, feel free to swap the red ink for one of these. It's also probably worth mentioning that you should leave a little longer between layers for paints to properly dry.

Step 1

First, we'll put a base colour down. We'll be using quite a lot of inks through this process, so you want something fairly bright, which will

also add a subtle shift to the subsequent tones. Again, the armour is already painted.

Brush Used	Paint
Size 2 round brush	Vallejo 803 Brown Rose

Step 2

Now, to make the tunic actually red, we'll use a red ink all over. Simply paint this on as a layer of paint, allowing it to catch and pool in the recesses. If you're using a homemade wash for this stage, you may need a little extra flow improver to really let the paint conform to the contours of the model's clothing.

Brush Used	Paint
Size 2 round brush	Vallejo Game Color Red Ink

Step 3

As Madder Red is a fairly rich colour, we'll give the model another wash, this time using purple. This will serve to tone back the garish red that is already on the figure. If you like the bright red, you can skip this step, or if you want a darker red, you can instead use a green or brown wash. When applying the wash, do so all over the model, but this time try to avoid overloading the brush or allowing the colour to pool at the edges of the garment.

Brush Used	Paint
Size 2 round brush	Army Painter Purple Tone

Step 4

To really emphasize the burgundy nature of the Madder Red, we'll add a highlight of the same base colour we used before starting to apply the inks. Red is a difficult colour to highlight, as it can very quickly lose it's 'redness', so be sparing with your highlights, only applying them to the most prominent areas. If you want to get a more orange or bolder red, use a scarlet or dark orange colour instead here.

Brush Used	Paint
Size 1 round brush	Vallejo 803 Brown Rose

6

Flesh Tones

By the beginning of the second century AD, the Roman Empire covered from Britain in the north, across Europe to the Black Sea, then south and east into the Middle East, along the North African Mediterranean coast and up again through modern-day Spain and Portugal.

To serve as a legionary, one had to have Roman citizenship. In the Early Imperial period, this would predominantly be limited to citizens of Italy and the Mediterranean basin. Legionaries would most frequently be recruited from the agricultural populations of wider Italy, as the legions' physical entry requirements were fairly stringent.

By restricting recruitment to citizens, however, one can quickly see a vast manpower shortage for providing security and force projection over an area as vast as the Roman Empire. To rectify this, the legions

were supported by auxiliary cohorts and cavalry drawn from *peregrinus*, subjects of the Empire who were not afforded citizenship status. These people made up the bulk of the Empire's population.

Under the Emperor Claudius, auxiliaries received a significant boost to their standing. In return for twenty-five years' service, they would be granted citizenship upon their retirement, as would their children. Auxilia were trained and equipped to the same high standards as their legionary colleagues, but provided different tactical roles, predominantly serving as light infantry, light and heavy cavalry, and archers.

Auxilia would typically serve far away from their home territories, so as to prevent the temptation for insurrection in their homelands. One of the more famous auxilia cohorts, one of Hamian archers, was recruited from modern-day Syria and eventually served in Britain. By the mid-second century, Britain contained more cohorts of auxilia than anywhere else in the Empire.

When painting your figures, you have a bit of freedom when it comes to their skin tones. Broadly speaking, legionaries will be pretty tanned, given both their pre-legion life and the amount of time spent engaged in training, exercises and marches once in the legion.

Auxilia, however, have a greater degree of flexibility. Given the fairly disparate range of environments from which they were recruited, you can cover a fairly wide variety of different skin tones in your auxilia units.

Skin, and especially faces, form the focal point of a figure. The eye is naturally drawn there when looking at a model. It would be quite easy to fill half this book discussing and demonstrating different flesh and face effects and details. However, as the focus is on getting armies down for gaming, I'll instead demonstrate a few quick and simple methods that will still look good, without taking an age to do, and are also suited to working with batch painting.

I prefer to paint the skin on a figure last, though some people like to do it first. For me, it's setting the character of the model and ends the process by bringing them to life. Plus, when using so many washes and dry brushing stages, it makes life infinitely easier. I'll also not be doing the eyes with pupils and irises, as this level of detail disappears in a massed unit, and instead will just finish them with a dot of Vallejo Game Colour Blue Ink.

TANNED SKIN

Step 1

For our tanned, weathered skin, we'll be starting with a deep, bronzed skin tone, though you can also use a light brown instead if you prefer. You'll need the basic skin tone to be pretty opaque, so you may require a few careful, thin coats rather than a single heavy, thick one.

Brush Used	Paint
Size 1 round brush	Vallejo 860 Medium Flesh

Step 2

There are a couple of options when it comes to shading tanned skin, with many pre-mixed flesh washes on the market. Here, though, we'll be doing something a little different, using either a green or purple shader, depending on the look you want to achieve. For a more olive-toned skin, we'll use the Military Shader from the Army Painter range. For a warmer-toned tan look, instead use a purple shade, in this case Purple Tone also from Army Painter. When applying your shade, try to prevent it being too thick and avoid pooling, especially on exposed areas like arms and legs.

Brush Used	Paint
Size I round brush	Army Painter Purple Tone or Military Shader

Step 3

To finish the flesh, we'll add a simple highlight, being careful to restrict it to the most prominent parts of the face, and also pick out the eyes with some Vallejo Game Colour Blue Ink. If you want to get your figures done quickly, you can of course skip this step.

Brush Used	Paint
Size I round brush	Vallejo 955 Flat Flesh
Size I round brush	Vallejo Game Colour Blue Ink

PALE SKIN

Step 1

If you want to do some paler-skinned figures, such as auxiliaries from somewhere in the Empire's northern territories, start with a medium, ruddy flesh colour, in this case Vallejo Brown Rose. As before, you want a nice opaque base, so may need to apply a few thin coats. If your figure has facial hair, apply a base colour to this now too.

Brush Used	Paint
Size 1 round brush	Vallejo 803 Brown Rose

Step 2

Now we add a first highlight, which will be applied to most of the face, allowing the previous layer to remain visible in all of the recesses. We'll use a lighter flesh tone that has a good contrast with the previous layer.

Brush Used	Paint
Size 1 round brush	Vallejo 815 Basic Skintone

Step 3

As previously mentioned, there are many different types of and colours of flesh wash on the market. However, I prefer something a little more vibrant, and will use a red tone wash instead. This is applied evenly all over the areas of the model's skin.

Brush Used	Paint
Size 1 round brush	Army Painter Red Tone

Step 4

At any of the previous three stages you can call the figure done, but a final highlight will really make the skin 'pop' visually, so we'll apply a very selective set of highlights to the most prominent, or raised, parts of the face using the same highlight colour as in step 2.

Brush Used	Paint
Size 1 round brush	Vallejo 815 Basic Skintone

DARK SKIN

Step 1

When painting darker skin tones, it's easy to over highlight and make them appear too pale or contrasted. We'll be aiming for a fairly natural appearance to the skin, starting with a medium brown, and then shading and highlighting to keep a subtle but convincing look.

Brush Used	Paint
Size 1 round brush	Vallejo 940 Saddle Brown

Step 2

When shading darker skin I use a purple, as this creates a richer, warmer colour. Alternatively, you can use a medium brown or red wash, depending on what you have to hand and personal preference.

Brush Used	Paint
Size 1 round brush	Army Painter Purple Tone

Step 3

For a highlight layer we need a fairly warm tone, and I prefer to make use of commercially available flesh tones for this. I'm only going to add one layer of highlight here, though if you wish you can add in more, or different tones, again depending on what you have to hand and personal taste. With this highlight, aim to be very selective, and only apply it to the most raised and prominent parts of the figure's skin.

Brush Used	Paint
Size 1 round brush	Vallejo 860 Medium Flesh

When it comes to painting skin on figures, there is a huge variety of flesh tone paints, washes and glazes for sale, including whole sets devoted to just skin tones. It can become a very complicated and detailed process, adding stubble, detailed eyes and different tones across a face, and a myriad of other techniques. Hopefully, the above will give you a few pointers into your own wider experiments, and also get a few models down on the table top.

7

Roman Cavalry; Painting Horses

Whilst the Early Imperial Roman military is predominantly perceived as an infantry army, cavalry still fulfilled a large and important role. The majority of the Roman cavalry component consisted of auxiliary units, though each legion also maintained 120 cavalrymen, who served in a largely reconnaissance and communications capacity, predominantly functioning as scouts and messengers.

Comprising the bulk of the Roman cavalry arm were the auxiliary cavalry. These were largely equipped in the same way as auxiliary infantry, wearing mail, helmets and oval or octagonal shields. They were also heavily armed, capable of wielding a short lance, bows or javelins, as well as a longer sword than their infantry colleagues, the *spatha*.

Auxiliary cavalry were organized into *alae* (essentially a regiment) of either 480 or 720 men. These would mostly be recruited from the Gallic, Germanic, Iberian and Thracian tribes subsumed into the Empire. The Romans did not have a stirrup to help with control of the horse, so relied upon rider skill to maintain control. This requisite level of skill and capability was rewarded with significantly higher daily pay than a legionary received.

Broadly speaking, in battle the Roman cavalryman was used to secure the armies' flanks, attack the flanks and rear of their enemies, and then pursue and ride down a defeated enemy.

In addition to these conventional cavalry, Rome also had several more specialized units of horsemen. Numidians (from North Africa), who had initially fought against Rome alongside Hannibal, came to provide very highly-regarded light cavalry forces. These *Equites Numidarum* were very lightly equipped, relying upon speed and agility to protect them, and served as excellent scouts and skirmishers.

At the other end of the spectrum, the Romans had encountered heavily armed and armoured elite caste cavalry of both the Sarmatians and Parthians during the Dacian and incessant Parthian wars. Being ever-accommodating to new ideas, during the reign of the Emperor Hadrian the *Equites Cataphractarii* begin to appear in Roman service (though they may have been present much earlier). These were very heavy shock cavalry, with both horse and rider wearing typically either mail or scale armour, wielding a long, two-handed lance. *Cataphractarii* would be formed in a solid, dense formation, and be used to deliver a shattering blow to an opposing battle line.

Perhaps the most famous Roman cavalry formation were the *Equites Singulares Augusti*, the elite cavalry arm of the Praetorian Guard. Based in Rome, the *Equites Singulares Augusti*'s primary role was the protection of the emperor. Armed and equipped along similar lines to other cavalry, they are notably portrayed on Trajan's Column carrying hexagonal shields, with their distinctive scorpion design. Recruitment was drawn from amongst already serving members of the cavalry auxilia.

Typically, the Romans seem to have used a horse close in size to a modern-day pony. These were stocky, short, but very strong animals, and from surviving frescos and mosaics were a variety of colours. For our cavalry, we'll cover black, grey and brown horses. Horses come in a fairly broad range of these colours, so we'll just use some middling tones. You can also use these same techniques on models wearing fur.

BROWN HORSE

We'll start off with a brown horse, specifically a chestnut brown. This is probably going to be the most common colour of horse you paint, though brown covers a fairly broad range of colour, ranging from almost black to a light sandy colour.

Step 1

Working over a black primer, paint all the horse with a fairly medium brown. Avoid getting any paint on the mane, tail and hooves. You can also leave part of the lower legs black.

Brush Used	Paint
Size 2 round brush	Vallejo 940 Saddle Brown

Step 2

To add both some richness to the horses tone, and add some easy shading, we'll use a deep brown wash. There are many available that would work: sepia tones, chestnuts and burnt umber are all good. If you have a lighter brown, you could use a less intense colour. Army Painter Soft Tone or Purple Tone, for example, work very well over light brown and tan colours. You can apply the wash to the tail and mane too.

Brush Used	Paint
Size 2 round brush	Vallejo Game Ink 093 Skin Wash

Step 3

You can leave your horse as it is now, or, if you want to go for some more detail, you can add a highlight. We're only going to add a fairly minimal amount of highlights, and use some heavily thinned paint only on the most prominent areas of the model. I've also used some Army Painter Dark Tone ink on the horse's mane and tail, and picked out the hooves with dark brown.

Brush Used	Paint
Size 1 round brush	Vallejo 891 Orange Brown.

GREY HORSE

Grey horses also come in a fairly broad range of tones, from near white to a fairly dark grey. To do a darker grey, you can use the same techniques as the brown horse, though substituting the brown with grey paint, and use a dark brown or black wash as a shader. Here, though, we'll do a very pale, almost white horse.

Step 1

As with before, paint all of the model, avoiding the saddle and straps. You may need a few thinner coats to get a solid colour here, as the base tone is going to be quite light. We'll use a light but warm grey colour as our base here. We can also add the mane and tail at this stage, using a darker yellow ochre colour.

Brush Used	Paint
Size 2 round brush	Vallejo 987 Medium Grey
Size 2 round brush	Vallejo 914 Green Ochre

Step 2

We'll do two layers of highlights on our grey horse, using heavily thinned paints at each stage. It doesn't matter too much if the contrast is subtle, as we can always go back over the highlights we add now before going on to the next step. Here, you want to add highlights to all the raised areas and areas that naturally catch the light. At the same time, use the same process to add highlights to the most prominent parts of the mane and tail.

Brush Used	Paint
Size 2 round brush	Vallejo 986 Deck Tan
Size 2 round brush	Vallejo 976 Buff

Step 3

We now add the final highlight to the horse. We're going to again use some heavily thinned paint, and apply it to the upper areas of the horse's body, the tops of muscles and prominent parts of the face. We'll do the same thing with the horses' tail and mane, adding the final highlight to the tip of the tail and most prominent parts of the mane. Here, we'll be using the same colour for both parts of the horse.

Brush Used	Paint
Size 1 round brush	Vallejo 837 Pale Sand

BLACK

Black horses are rarely actually jet black, most often being a very dark brown. With our horse we'll start painting it brown, highlighting it, and then darkening the horse's colours back down again with a wash. We'll finish with an optional final, stark highlight.

Step 1

As our horse is already primed black, we can go straight to adding a highlight. Using a very dark brown, apply this selectively to the most prominent parts of the animal and the uppermost parts of its body. You can use the same colour for the mane and tail here too.

Brush Used	Paint
Size 2 round brush	Vallejo 822 German Camouflage Black Brown

Step 2

We'll add some very precise and careful highlights now, ensuring that the highlight is limited to the uppermost areas, very lightly to catch the light. Ensure your paint is very thin, not much thicker than a wash. If the highlights don't seem to stand out much, then that's perfectly fine.

Brush Used	Paint
Size 2 round brush	Vallejo 987 Medium Grey

Step 3

We'll now start to make the horse look black by applying a black wash all over the model. Try not to let it pool, but do ensure you cover the whole figure, as you want to make everything darker.

Brush Used	Paint
Size 2 round brush	Army Painter Dark Tone

Step 4

You can call your horse done now, or if you want to give it a shiny, glossy look, we can add another highlight. You could alternatively carefully dry brush some gloss varnish onto the horse. For now though, we'll simply apply a very neat, careful and precise highlight on only the very highest and most prominent of details.

Brush Used	Paint
Size 1 round brush	Vallejo 987 Medium Grey

With all of these, we can pick out the horse's eyes with some black ink and the hooves with whatever dark grey or dark brown you happen to prefer. Whilst these guides have been prepared with horses in mind, the Roman military used the hides of various large, predatory animals in the panoply of specialists, notably standard bearers and musicians. These guides can be used or tweaked to fit those too.

LEATHER

Most of the models in your army, not just the cavalry, will have some form of leather harness. Typically, these would be a dark brown or black, though we also see quite a lot of red in contemporary frescos and mosaics.

BROWN LEATHER

For our brown leather, we want a dark, dull brown, and will do this very quickly and simply. Buckles can be painted using the techniques covered in the section of this book covering armour and metals.

Step 1

Very simple this; just pick out your straps with a layer of dark brown.

Brush Used	Paint
Size 1 round brush	Vallejo 871 Leather Brown

Step 2

As there's not too much to the straps, a quick layer of dark brown wash will serve to accentuate the detail and create a dark border between the strap and surrounding model.

Brush Used	Paint
Size 1 round brush	Army Painter Strong Tone

Step 3

If you want to further emphasize the detail, add some very crisp highlights to the upper edges and corners of straps. If you want to have the leather appear a little more worn and cracked, paint a rougher edge and small lines across the strap to give the impression of wear and fraying.

Brush Used	Paint
Size 1 round brush	Vallejo 914 Green Ochre

RED STRAPPING

Red straps are even easier to paint. I'd save these for adding to important figures, such as officers or standard bearers, though there doesn't seem to be much in the way of consistency of colour here historically. I've added it to the tack of one of my line cavalry man, as the red will be a nice contrast to his black horse.

Step 1

Paint the straps with a very dark red, leaving some of the black primer showing in the deepest recesses, and use the metal guide to pick out any buckles.

Brush Used	Paint
Size 1 round brush	Vallejo 859 Black Red

Step 2

All we need now is a very simple highlight. Using some thinned down bright red, go over most of the strap, leaving the darker red visible in areas of natural shade or deep recess. Once dry, come back and add another layer of this same highlight if your red is looking too muted for your tastes.

Brush Used	Paint
Size 1 round brush	Vallejo 817 Scarlet

With that, we have some basics covered for painting horses, animals and leather work. Painting a unit of cavalry can be a fairly arduous process, but hopefully these guides will help you get through them easily. If you want to liven things up, you also have the option of varying each horse's colours. Alternatively, you could aim to paint them as a batch using the same colour for all of them. The riders' uniforms and equipment will serve to give the group a visually unified appearance anyway, so you have a little freedom either way to tailor the painting of their mounts to your own preferences.

8

Basing

With an area as vast as the Roman Empire, the terrain your models would have fought over stretches all the way from the forests of Dacia to Iberian plains and the deserts of Egypt.

Bases are the most practical and heavily used part of the figure, being picked up, pushed around and generally nudged frequently when in use. Despite this, they also give you a lot of scope to bring your army to life and illustrate the story of where it is fighting.

The basing of your models serves as a framework to their paint job, and can help to make a really striking, coherent-looking army. With ancient

armies, you'll sometimes use bases with more than one figure on, while others will be individually based models. With both of these, my preference is to attach the model to the base before doing the scenic work.

I'll present guides to doing arid, grass and snow bases, as these should cover the majority of environments your figures will be posted to. The first stage is always to add some texture to the base, which serves to blend the figure into the base and add some initial interest to bare wood or plastic. The two most popular ways to do this are to glue sand to the base and then paint it, or to use a texture paint. I'll be using a textured paint, as this is a little quicker and simpler.

GREEN BASE

Grassy, green bases are probably the most common and popular of gaming bases, and can fit in most board and terrain collections. My preferred method is to use a selection of static grasses applied in clumps, but patches of pre-made tufts are also popular. You can opt to have patches of earth showing through the grass too, which can be enhanced by simply doing a quick dry brush over the base colour of the texture paint before attaching your chosen foliage.

Static grass is, as the name suggests, scenic grass. It typically comes provided in bags and looks best when you use a few different lengths and colours, as we'll show here. Also popular for basing is clump foliage, provided as small, suitably coloured pieces of foam, which work very well as a base before applying static grass over the top to add more texture and depth to your ground cover.

Tufts are very similar to static grass, though are perhaps a little easier to apply. Tufts can also provide some fantastic details like bushes or flowers. Typically, they consist of a small cluster of grass or flowers that are carried on a backing sheet. The tuft is then lifted from the backing sheet and glued to the model.

Step 1

The base has been painted with Vallejo 26.218 Earth Texture acrylic, and left to dry. We'll now add a little depth to the effect by giving it a dry brushing with a lighter earth tone. Be careful of your figure's feet, though if you do go over them simply neaten them up before going onto step 2

Brush Used	Paint
Size 2 angled brush	Vallejo 825 German Camouflage Pale Brown

Step 2

For the rest of these steps we'll be using an old, worn brush. The size doesn't matter too much. A pair of tweezers will also be handy; again the size of them doesn't really matter.

To start adding the ground work to our base, we'll paint a few patches of diluted PVA glue onto the base, then use our tweezers to pick up some clump foliage and apply that to the PVA areas.

Step 3

If you want to add some details like flowers or shrubs, again do some patches of PVA and add some tufts that fit the theme you like the look of. Here I've used both shrubs and flowers. I've used some that fit the colours already on the base, but they can be a good way to add some contrasting colours if you so wish.

Step 4

In this final stage, we add the static grass. Again, paint some patches of PVA onto the base. Then, using your tweezers, apply clumps of your first type of static grass. The PVA takes a little while to dry, so you can repeat this process a few times, adding more and more depth and variety to your grasses, depending how many you have to hand.

Several types of green will give you a spring or summer feel, though mixing increasing amounts of brown and straw colours will enhance an autumnal tone. For this one, I've used a short green, a longer dark green and a short dark brown colour.

SNOW BASE

Snow bases can be amongst the most striking and visually impressive you can do. They also set an easy tone and narrative to a collection, even if they are a little restrictive in their setting and require specialized scenery to really look the part. Whilst you can go straight to simply covering the base in snow, and this can have its place, I'm going to do a patchy snow layer over some dead grass.

The initial part of this is essentially the same as with a grass base, but instead of green tones, we'll use a few different types of brown and straw-coloured grass to enhance the dead of winter atmosphere. Once you've done this, leave the base to dry, preferably overnight. If you're planning on using a spray varnish on your models, it's also worth doing this now, before adding the snow.

Step 1
Here I've made a base in a very similar style to the green base, though I've kept it a little simpler, and used longer lengths of brown and green. I wanted to get the feel of an untended winter meadow.

Step 2
Adding snow is actually very easy, and there are some good snow effect commercial products on the market. A cheaper option, though, is to use bicarbonate of soda and some water effect. Though there are some

concerns about the bicarb going yellow with age, the water effect serves to seal and protect it.

To add the snow, simply paint some fairly thick patches of water effect onto the areas you'd like to add snow to, then just sprinkle your bicarb onto the water effect. To do this, I just grab a pinch and apply it to the water effect before it dries. You can use a cocktail stick to mix the bicarb into the water effect if you like, and then sprinkle on a little more bicarb to get a denser look to your snow.

ARID BASE

There are a few different types of arid base you can go for: deep desert, hot summer or rocky scrubland, to name but three. Here we'll go for a scrubland appearance, as this can then be used as a jumping-off point for any sort of arid look you may want.

Step 1

As with the previous types of base, we'll start with a textured base layer: you could use fine sand and not paint it, however I find that tends to look a little heavy, more like gravel when compared to the size of our models. Instead, my preference again is to use textured paint, this time Vallejo 26.217 Sand. Alternatively to this, there are several very nice cracked-earth effect paints available that represent heat-broken

earth. I've given this a dry brush of pale sand to help emphasize the texture we've added.

Brush Used	Paint
Size 2 angled brush	Vallejo 837 Pale Sand

Step 2

I want to give the impression of rocky, rough ground, and to do this we'll add some PVA to the base and then sprinkle on some gravel. If you can, mixing two or three different types and colours of gravel would be ideal. Once the glue is dry, give the base a quick dry brush with a light sand colour. You don't need to be too heavy with this; just enough to pick out the detail will suffice.

Brush Used	Paint
Size 2 angled brush	Vallejo 837 Pale Sand

Step 3

To further pull the colours together, we'll give the base a wash. If you want to go for a more desert sand effect, I'd suggest using an ochre colour; however, for a dry earth, I'd instead go for a more neutral brown. In this case, for the scrubland effect, we'll use the neutral brown. Apply the wash with an old brush; the size and shape is unimportant, though you want one big enough to get a decent flow to the paint when you

apply it. I've heavily thinned down some light brown paint with water, and applied it as a wash.

Brush Used	Paint
Size 2 old brush	Vallejo 825 German Camouflage Pale Brown

Step 4

If you want to go for a deep desert effect, you can simply leave your bases as they are now. However, I'd like to give them some scrub plants. To do this, we'll apply some PVA glue in random patches, then add some green clump foliage. Whilst the glue is still wet, we'll add some straw static grass. You could alternatively simply use a suitable ready-made tuft if you prefer.

Basing

Basing may appear somewhat time-consuming, but all of these steps are fairly quick and easy to do, especially with a movie on in the back ground! It's worth investing in a few different types of static grass or tufts, and simply grabbing ones you like the look of. I'd also suggest writing a note inside the container of what it's called, and where you got it from, to make future basing material purchases easer. It can be most frustrating when you run out part way through …

With a bit of forwards planning, and selective use of complimentary colours, you can come up with some really impressive ground work to make your collection spectacular.

Appendix A

Manufacturers List

The Early Imperial Roman period probably has a greater, more varied range of models than anything else, except perhaps Second World War German. The accuracy and quality can vary significantly, as can the price. It's always worth doing a quick search online and perusing catalogues before ordering, to get a good idea of what is available.

With so many manufactures, I've attempted to be as exhaustive as I can, but there will inevitably be some that I've overlooked or forgotten, and to those I apologize. I've also listed a few manufactures of specifically Roman scenery, and a few decal sources too.

Size: 28mm	Notes:
Warlord Games	Warlord produce an extensive range of plastic and metal figures. Plastic unit boxes also contain shield decals.
Victrix Limited	Wide range of plastic figures, and also some very nice shield transfers.
Aventine Miniatures	Wide range of ancients, including an extensive line of Early Imperial Romans.
1st Corps	Metal figures and good unit deals.
Essex Miniatures	Wide range of metal figures.
Crusader Miniatures	Crusader have a range of metal Romans, including gladiators.
Black Tree Design	Extensive ranges of metal figures, with frequent sale offers.
Steve Barber Models	A range of civilians and also a fort.
Footsore Miniatures	At the time of writing, an extensive range of civilians for the Gangs of Rome game.

Old Glory	Metal figures.
Wargames Foundry	Very wide range of metal figures.

Size: 20mm	Notes:
HaT	Soft plastic range, covering most types of Roman soldier.
Caesar	Very extensive range of plastic Romans. The name might be a giveaway!
Esci	Small range, also sold by Italeri, of soft plastic figures.
Strelets	Another large and varied range of soft plastic figures.
Zvezda	Plastic figures.
Airfix	Very old set; good for nostalgia though.
Revell	Fairly dated range in soft plastic.
Italeri	Soft plastic figures.

Size: 15mm	Notes:
AB	Small but beautiful metal range. Good selection of less often available things such as wagons.
War and Empire	Very large and extensive metal range. Very nice models, and a big range of terrain too.
Essex	Range of metal figures.
Old Glory	Metal figures.
1st Corps	Metal figures.
Xyston miniatures	Wide range of metal models, requiring some minor assembly.
Totentanz Miniatures	Very nice range of metal figures.
Irregular Miniatures	Can select individual figures.
Baueda Miniatures	Good range of metal models, and very nice camp accessories.

Magister Militum	Metal figures.
Rebel Miniatures	Metal range of figures.

Size: 10mm and smaller	
Steve Barber Models	10mm metal.
Pendraken Miniatures	10mm metal.
Magister Militum	10mm metal.
Irregular Miniatures	10mm metal.
Baccus Miniatures	6mm metal figures.
Irregular Miniatures	6mm metal.

Terrain	
Sarrissa Precision	A wide range of 28mm MDF Roman buildings, especially town and villa pieces.
Warbases	Extensive range of 15mm MDF Roman buildings, very reasonably priced.
Timeline Miniatures	A selection of MDF Roman fortifications, in a variety of scales.
Grand Manner	Wide range of resin items, including ships.
War and Empire	15mm resin buildings.
Leven Miniatures	6mm resin buildings.

The Roman legionary is probably the most recognizable and iconic fighting man of all time. Extremely well-equipped, well-trained and sent to the far-flung corner of the Roman Empire, he has become a perennial favourite with modellers, wargamers and collectors.

Entering into the world of collecting a wargaming force of the ancient world can appear a daunting task: the myriad clothing, armour and equipment can appear overwhelming, while deciphering how to paint and model this can put an end to a project before it even begins.

To help you turn those dreams of legions into reality, this book aims to guide the novice hobbyist through their first steps of selecting glues,

paints and tools, and on to painting the armour, clothing, shields, horses and skin tones of the Roman military in the Early Imperial period. The book is rounded off with a guide to bringing the models' bases to life, and a list of manufacturers of models, transfers and scenery.

Andy Singleton is an experienced, professional painter, specializing in getting massed collections together quickly. With this book, he uses his years of experience to guide you through the process of putting together an attractive Roman army for the tables of your campaigns.

List of Models Used

Through the course of producing this book, I've used miniatures from a range of manufacturers. I have compiled a list of these by chapter in the following lists. All figures used in the guides in this book were 28mm-sized.

1. **Front cover and foreword**
   Warlord Games
   Primus Pilus
   Early Imperial Romans plastic Roman legionaries

2. **Tools of the Trade**
   Depot Battalion by Colonel Bills
   Early Imperial Roman cart crew
   Medium-sized cart
   Draught oxen
   Early Imperial Roman weapons and supplies

   Warlord Games
   Early Imperial Roman Aquilifer
   Early Imperial Romans Praetorian Guard
   Early Imperial Romans Auxilliary regiment
   Ancient Celts Celtic Warriors boxed set
   Early Imperial Romans Civilians
   Early Imperial Romans Officers
   Unleash Hell!

   Wargames Foundry
   IRO83 Emperor Vespasian

3. **Early Imperial Romans Weapons and Armour**
   Warlord Games
   Early Imperial Romans Auxilliary regiment
   Early Imperial Romans plastic Roman legionaries
   Early Imperial Romans Scorpion

   Wargames Foundry
   IRO83 Emperor Vespasian
   IRO31 Imperial Roman Command 1

   Victrix Limited
   Early Imperial Roman legionaries advancing

4. **Shields**
   Warlord Games
   Early Imperial Romans plastic Roman legionaries
   Ancient Celts Celtic Warriors boxed set
   Early Imperial Romans Auxilliary regiment

5. **Tunics, Helmet Crests and Cloaks**
   Warlord Games
   Early Imperial Romans Civilians
   Ancient Celts army standard bearer
   Early Imperial Roman Aquilifer
   Early Imperial Roman Auxiliary Cavalry with spears

   Wargames Foundry
   IRO83 Emperor Vespasian

   Victrix Limited
   Early Imperial Roman legionaries advancing

6. **Flesh tones**
   Footsore Miniatures
   Slave Mob

Wargames Foundry
IRO83 Emperor Vespasian

Victrix Limited
Early Imperial Roman legionaries advancing

Warlord Games
Early Imperial Romans Auxilliary regiment
Early Imperial Romans plastic Roman legionaries

7. **Roman cavalry painting horses**
   Warlord Games
   Early Imperial Roman Auxiliary Cavalry with spears

8. **Basing**
   Warlord Games
   Early Imperial Roman Medicus
   Early Imperial Romans plastic Roman legionaries

In addition to the above ranges of figures, the following buildings were also used in several photographs:

Warbases
28mm Dark Age range
Grub Hut
Timber Barn
Viking Longhouse
Watchtower

Timeline Miniatures
28mm Roman Fort front